From
A to **Z**
A Folk Art Alphabet

From A to Z
A Folk Art Alphabet

Karen M. Jones

THE MAIN STREET PRESS

Pittstown, New Jersey

Published by The Main Street Press, Inc.
William Case House
Pittstown, New Jersey 08867

Published simultaneously in Canada by Methuen Publications
2330 Midland Avenue
Agincourt, Ontario M1S 1P7

Designed by Al Cetta
Printed in the United States of America

Library of Congress Cataloging in Publication Data

Jones, Karen M., 1948-
From A to Z, a folk art alphabet.

  Summary: A series of American folk art pictures
from the eighteenth and nineteenth centuries
accompanied by the letters of the alphabet.
  1. Folk art—United States. 2. Primitivism in
art—United States. 3. Alphabets. [1. Folk art—
United States. 2. Alphabet] I. Title.
NK805.J66 1985   745'.0973   85-4954
ISBN 0-915590-65-4 (pbk.)

Introduction

The works of art reproduced on these pages represent the merest sampling from the enormously rich and varied body of American folk art that has been unearthed, assessed, and applauded in the past fifty years, and the selection only hints at the diversity of subjects and mediums that served as tools of artistic expression.

The art created by and for the common people of post-Revolutionary America is characterized by a freshness and candor that distinguish it from the work of American masters who were painting formal portraits and landscapes for wealthy patrons in frank imitation of European academic art. Many folk artists were acquainted with the work of their academic counterparts in America and had probably seen European paintings reproduced in books and engravings. Some were sign and coach painters; others were craftsmen, such as weather-vane makers and carvers; still others were women whose talents are reflected in decorative household furnishings. They were largely self-taught, and their ambition was to record the appearance of familiar people and objects or to enhance the beauty of their surroundings, rather than to achieve a high degree of technical proficiency. Their work is never awe inspiring, but is sometimes majestic; it is often complex, but never pretentious.

The names of many of the artists whose work appears here are unknown. Some probably earned their livings largely or solely by their art; others were talented amateurs who created pictures for their own enjoyment. The ones whose stories we know provide a fascinating insight into the personalities behind the art.

Jonathan Fisher, a preacher, school teacher, skilled craftsman, and inventor, read Hebrew, Greek, Latin, and French. He painted twenty-two known oils of various subjects and engraved over 140 wood blocks of animals, birds, reptiles, and insects mentioned in the Bible for a volume entitled *Scripture Animals,* which in his words was "designed especially to assist young people in gaining a knowledge of the natural history of the Bible." His large-folio watercolor sketchbook of exotic and commonplace plants and animals is here represented by *The Great Horned Owl from Athens* and *The Male Zebra.*

The reclusive Mary Ann Willson, whose *Marimaid* inexplicably flourishes a bow and arrow, defied convention in her way of life as well as in her art. According to one account, she and the woman with whom she lived had "experienced a romance that had broken their hearts," and they moved from Connecticut to the wilderness of Greene County, New York, "seeking peace and forgetfulness." The subjects of her known watercolors include portraits and Biblical scenes, and she is reported to have sold a great many paintings "from Canada to Mobile."

The little we know about Joshua Johnston has been embellished by legends handed down through the families of his subjects. He is listed in Baltimore directories as a portraitist from 1796 to 1824 and is the first black man known to have painted professionally. He was probably initially a slave, but from 1817 his name is found in directories under "Free Householders of Color," which has led to speculation that he bought his freedom with income from his painting. Descendants of the subject of one of his portraits believe that he was once a valet to the Peale family, and the portrait of the baby holding a branch of cherries, which is attributed to Johnston, does bear some affinity to portraits by that prolific dynasty of painters.

According to family tradition, the German immigrant Jacob Maentel was educated as a physician and served as a secretary to Napoleon. In this country Maentel was a farmer whose sensitive watercolor portraits, exemplified by the amusing *Boy with Rooster*, attest his true vocation.

The subjects of folk portraits often posed with their pets, and the preponderance of animals in likenesses of early Americans is testimony to the esteem in which the family mascot was held. Dogs gaze up lovingly at their masters or peer out deferentially from under tables; cats rest unwillingly or dangle uncomfortably in the arms of children; and birds perch on fingers and chair backs. Occasionally household pets were themselves dignified in portraiture. The dog in the garden and the cat with her kittens were clearly deemed worthy subjects, and *The Horse with the Longest Mane and Tail in the World* tells his own story.

The German-speaking peoples who settled in southeastern Pennsylvania beginning in the late seventeenth century brought with them a distinctive Old World tradition of decoration, several examples of which are pictured here. The illuminated manuscripts and documents produced largely by schoolmasters and their pupils in the eighteenth and first half of the nineteenth century form the most cohesive group of works by American folk artists. Known collectively as Fraktur for the Gothic script in which much of the textual material is written, they were embellished with vigorous drawings of birds, animals, flowers, hearts, and geometric motifs. The eagle and star, from a *Taufschein*, or baptismal certificate, are painted in the bright, pure colors that typify the best examples. The roses and tulips are purely pictorial drawings, unaccompanied by any text, but done in the Fraktur style. Durs Rudy's drawing of Jesus and the disciples at Galilee is an unusual example of Fraktur whose theme is taken directly from a passage in the Bible.

Fraktur artists sometimes turned their hand to ornamenting furniture with the same stylized, imaginatively drawn motifs that appear on illuminated manuscripts. The unicorn from a blanket chest of 1788 may be an example of this practice.

The circular cutout valentine, or *Liebesbrief,* had been made by Pennsylvania Germans as early as 1770 and preceded common use of lacelike valentines by Anglo-Americans by decades. The valentine made for Dinah McFadgen incorporates familiar Pennsylvania-German motifs.

Among America's earliest commercial artists were the painters of the tavern signs that advertised havens along the young nation's well-traveled turnpikes. William Rice's imposing lions must have gladdened the heart of many a bedraggled sojourner. *General Washington on a White Charger* is executed in the sign-painter's technique, but its use may simply have been ornamental.

Nowhere is the American folk artist's strong sense of design more apparent than in the work of women and artisans whose ingenuity elevated humble objects to distinctive works of art. The striking pattern of the alphabet quilt might have been intended to acquaint a child with his ABC's. The flag gate, Indian archer weather vane, and Neptune paddle wheel are three commanding statements of artistic expression.

The important role played by the female academies that flourished in nineteenth-century America in encouraging amateur artists is revealed in the freehand and stenciled still lifes and flower pieces that abound in collections of American folk art. In addition to the predictable academic curriculum, students were offered instruction in the rudiments of drawing and watercolor painting. Women continued to use the skills they had developed after they left the academies to create so-called fancy pieces to ornament their homes or to give to friends. Some ladies living in Rochester, New York, in the mid-nineteenth century turned their leisure-time activities to profit by executing plates for D. M. Dewey's horticultural sample book, here represented by the *Northern Spy Apple, Persimmon,* and *Purple Wistaria.* Students were encouraged to copy freely from prints and from widely circulated art-instruction books which offered pictures of animals, fruits, and other familiar objects. The very simple *Kitten Playing with Red Ball* may have been sketched as an exercise, but the artist's personal touches give it great charm.

Authors of ABC books in the past did not have an opportunity to choose from the colorful outpouring of naïve art which began in America after the Revolution and continued into the late nineteenth century. Like earlier alphabet books, *From A to Z* may, indeed, be useful as a teaching tool. If so, it will succeed because of the evocative quality of the art. The intent of the book—for children of all ages—is to lead the reader into a wider world of imaginative expression.

Some of the qualities that make the pictures in this folk-art alphabet so appealing are also to be found in the work of the largely anonymous illustrators of the ABC books through which our forebears became acquainted with the first of the three r's. The earliest of these volumes, however, appear rather grim to modern sensibility. They were illustrated by extremely crude woodcuts which reiterated the stern religious texts. The venerable *New-England Primer,* first published in Boston between 1687 and 1690, was the most universally studied primer in America for the next one-hundred years, and it has been conservatively estimated that during that period some three million copies were sold. Its rhymed alphabet of "moral and instructive" verses chiefly addressed to the topics of death and damnation was illustrated by very primitive drawings. Yet, notwithstanding the harrowing themes, there is in both verse and illustration an engaging simplicity which is reminiscent of the unsophisticated imagery found on Puritan gravestones.

About 1790 the *New-England Primer* took what the Calvinists must have felt was a turn for the worse: an edition appeared with an alphabet of verses illustrated by pictures of animals. This was the first bid for popularity among children, and it signaled the decline of the forbidding ecclesiastical texts that had predominated. It was also about this time that Noah Webster's *American Spelling Book* appeared. Though it was no less pedagogic than its predecessors, it contained several amusing fables and stories illustrated by relatively accomplished, beguiling pictures of animals and homely folk.

The turn of the century saw a refreshing proliferation of alphabet books that frankly attempted to make the lessons go down easier. The Free Library of Philadelphia has among its rich collection of children's literature a set of diminutive alphabet cards dating from about 1800, whose wry verses are accompanied by delightfully childlike and, most unusually, hand-tinted illustrations.

Although the shift from ecclesiastical to secular subjects in the school books of the nineteenth century opened an almost unlimited field of subjects that might be used to represent the letters of the alphabet, writers and illustrators of ABC books almost universally got stuck on some of them. Charles Dickens's description of the books that appeared under his Christmas tree when he was a young boy also speaks for those circulating in America at the time: "Thin books, in themselves, at first, but many of them, with deliciously smooth covers of bright red and green. What fat black letters to begin with! 'A was an archer, and shot at a frog.' Of course he was. He was an apple-pie also and there he is! He was a good many things in his time, was A, and so were most of his friends, except X, who had so little versatility that I never knew him to get beyond Xerxes or Xantippe; like Y, who was always confined to a yacht or a yew-tree, and Z, condemned forever to be a zebra or a zany." The unknown compiler of *The Poetic Gift: Or Alphabet in Rhyme*, which was published in New Haven in 1844, was plainly apologetic for his lack of inspiration: "Y and Z will end this list; My next shall be a better."

Allowing for the occasional lapse, these books are a delight to leaf through. The verses are often whimsical, and the illustrations ingenuous. In seeking to address the interests of their readers, they, like the folk art of the time, are reflective of the tastes and customs of the common people of America.

From apple to zebra, the subjects presented here owe their timeless appeal in part to their simplicity and familiarity and in part to the manner in which they were interpreted. The accomplished folk artist, often far removed from sophisticated centers of culture, captured intentionally or not the intrinsic beauty of everyday objects and freely adapted traditional symbols. In the personal touches—the oddly placed Z on the alphabet quilt, a mermaid holding a bow and arrow—we are reminded of the endless resourcefulness of the individual spirit in imparting to ordinary images an extraordinary vitality.

This book owes a great deal to the scholars who have examined and defined American folk art in publications and exhibitions over the years, but specific credit must be given to Alice Winchester, whose *Versatile Yankee* provided the background on Jonathan Fisher, and to N.F. Karlins, from whose article in *Antiques* for November 1976 the biographical information about Mary Ann Willson is taken. I am particularly grateful to Charles van Ravenswaay, whose *A Nineteenth-Century Garden* was the source for information about Dellon Marcus Dewey's horticultural sample book, for graciously permitting me to publish three plates from his collection; to Howell J. Heaney and the staff of the rare-book division of the Free Library of Philadelphia, who cheerfully and patiently guided me through the Rosenbach Collection of Early American Children's Books and provided a selection of Fraktur for publication herein; and to Margaret Moody of the Shelburne Museum, who supplied information about the mysterious inscription on the Indian archer weather vane.

—Karen M. Jones

From **A** to **Z**

A Folk Art Alphabet

NORTHERN SPY APPLE.

Apple

A word fitly spoken is like apples of gold in pictures of silver.
—Noah Webster, *American Spelling Book*, 1793

In 1859 Dellon Marcus Dewey, a Rochester, New York, bookseller and publisher with an interest in horticulture and art, produced a sample book of hand-colored illustrations of fruits, flowers, and ornamental trees. His was among the earliest issues of plates intended for use by so-called tree peddlers, who traveled throughout rural America selling plants to farmers and villagers for major nurseries. The original designs for these idealized pictures of native and imported varieties were either adapted from published sources or drawn from nature. Many were hand colored by women who had also created freehand and stenciled flower paintings to ornament the walls of their homes with the same crisp lines and clear colors that characterize Dewey's *Northern Spy Apple*. This is not a precisely accurate scientific rendering, but, rather, a personal interpretation of a native American species.

Northern Spy Apple from D. M. Dewey, *The Colored Fruit Book for the Use of Nurserymen*, Rochester, New York, c. 1859, lithograph outline with applied color, $11\frac{5}{16} \times 8\frac{5}{8}$ inches. *Courtesy, Charles van Ravenswaay.*

Baby

Cry, baby, cry,
Put your finger in your eye,
And tell your mother it wasn't I.

　　—Nursery rhyme, 1853

Folk portraitists often imbued their subjects with a personality lacking in the more accomplished works of their academic counterparts, and their depictions are sometimes less than flattering. In the baby's stern, pudgy face there is a hint of defiance, and one wonders how difficult a time the artist had in subduing her to sit for a likeness. The portrait is attributed to Joshua Johnston, a black man who is believed to be the first of his race to paint professionally. The artist was clearly an accomplished colorist; the flesh tones are realistic, and the shading is done with some subtlety. The baby's bead necklace and the lace trim on her dress are picked out with an economy of brushwork, and the stark contrast of the white gown against the dark background is brightened by the centrally placed branch of cherries in her determined fist.

Margaret Moore (?), attributed to Joshua Johnston, c. 1812, oil on canvas, 21 x 16⅞ inches. *Abby Aldrich Rockefeller Folk Art Center.*

Cat

The Cat does play,
And after slay.
　　—*New-England Primer,* c. 1688

There is little doubt that this cat and her kittens were household pets who were carefully observed and lovingly recorded. Each has a distinct personality, and certainly the kitten playing with the yarn knows he's gotten himself into a tangle. The lifelike colors and strong markings, particularly on the reclining kitten, evince the artist's command of palette and brush, and the overall composition is well balanced. No less care was given to the details of the wallpaper and baseboard molding in the background and the lace-trimmed curtain to the left. Through this attention to detail, which characterizes American folk painting, we are given a glimpse of the interior of a late nineteenth-century home in which the playful and the domestic are equally celebrated.

Cat and Kittens, artist unknown, 1872-1883, oil on millboard, 12 x 13⅞ inches. *National Gallery of Art.*

Dog

D stands for the Dog; and he's nobody's fool,
Although he has never been sent to school.

> —Francis Channing Woodworth,
> *The Picture A. B. C. Book,* c. 1850

The dog was a popular subject of folk painters in the nineteenth century and is often found in contemporary juvenile literature as an example of loyalty, bravery, and obedience. We might easily ascribe these attributes to this imperial canine who appears in gigantic proportion to the orderly garden in which he stands. Some of the bright flowers are identifiable as anemones, calla lilies, and varieties of daisy. The artist's appreciation of pattern and design is expressed in the symmetrically arranged semicircular plantings along the carefully delineated brick wall in the background.

The Dog, artist unknown, mid-nineteenth century, oil on canvas, 35¼ x 41½ inches. *National Gallery of Art.*

Eagle

The Eagle is of birds the king,
And soars on high with outstretched wing.
— Alphabet card, c. 1800

The eagles found on many of the Fraktur drawings of the
Pennsylvania Germans may have had their origins in European
heraldry and in some cases were adapted from the Great Seal of the
United States. The designer of this example had little concern for
either tradition, however, and posed his wide-eyed bird with what
appears to be an olive branch, which we might have expected to find
in the clutches of a dove rather than an eagle. The intricate feather
motif in bright hues of red and green interlaced with delicate strokes
of gold inspired one scholar of Pennsylvania-German art to refer to
this considerably talented decorator as the "Flying Pineapple Artist."

Detail of a *Taufschein*, probably Northampton County, Pennsylvania, c. 1820,
watercolor and ink on laid paper. *Free Library of Philadelphia*.

Flag

There is the National flag. He must be cold, indeed, who can look upon its folds rippling in the breeze without pride of country.

—Charles Sumner, "Are We a Nation?", 1867

While craftsmen often ornamented utilitarian objects, surely one of the more unusual examples of art applied to a mundane form is this flag gate from a farm in upper New York State. The number of stars in the field indicate that the gate was made after Colorado was admitted to the Union as the thirty-eighth state in 1876, and the exuberantly patriotic theme may have been inspired by the commemoration of the nation's centennial. Instead of arranging the stars in rows, as was commonly done on the official national flag, the artisan laid them out in an attractive elliptical pattern. From a distance the undulating stripes might have created the illusion of a flag waving in the wind.

Flag gate from the Darling Farm, Jefferson County, New York, c. 1876, painted wood and metal, width 56 inches. *Museum of American Folk Art, New York City.*

George Washington

*There are features in his face totally different from what I
ever observed in that of any other human being; the sockets of
the eyes, for instance, are larger, and the upper part of the
nose broader . . . yet his judgment and great self-command
make him appear a man of a different cast in the eyes
of the world.* —Gilbert Stuart, c. 1797

The strong sentiment occasioned by George Washington's death in 1799
expressed itself in commercial and popular art, and he endured as a
symbol of the republic well into the nineteenth century. The face of
George Washington on a White Charger was probably adapted from one of
the thousands of prints drawn from life portraits of Washington that
were circulated throughout the country. As we know from
Washington's adopted son George Washington Parke Custis, "In 1789
the first president lost all his teeth," and his grim expression in many
of the later portraits, and subsequent prints, is partly owing to the
resultant disfiguration. In this imposing portrait the general's
impassive, wan visage is almost lost amid the gay colors of his uniform
and the horse's trappings. The strong, flatly applied colors and the
linear quality of the figures are characteristic of early American shop
and tavern signs, and the unlikely scrolling floral vine on the saddle
and blanket further hints of the artist's penchant for decoration.

General Washington on a White Charger, artist unknown, 1800-1840,
oil on wood panel, 38½ x 29⅜ inches. *National Gallery of Art.*

Horse

H is a Horse who often kicks
and prances on the lawn.
*　　—The Poetic Gift:*
*　　　or Alphabet in Rhyme*, 1844

The Horse with the Longest Mane and Tail in the World may seem to have been the product of an artist's fancy, but legend has it that he was a real horse, owned by Martin E. Williams, a veterinarian in Chatham, New York, who showed the marvelous steed at fairs and horse shows. Arrayed in his silvery tresses, he gives the appearance of an overdressed pony and must have created a sensation among the country folk who visited the affairs where he was exhibited. The landscape and sky and the shading and highlights of the horse's hide are evidence of the influence of more formal painting on the folk artists of the time.

The Horse with the Longest Mane and Tail in the World,
artist unknown, c. 1890, oil on wood/panel, 18 × 24 inches.
New York State Historical Association, Cooperstown, New York.

Indian

I was an Indian,
with an arrow and bow.

—The First Blossoms
of Learning, c. 1835

Crouched atop a roof in rural Pennsylvania, this Indian archer weather vane must have formed a striking silhouette against the sky. The figure was chiseled out of a single sheet of iron and riveted onto an iron panel pierced with the mysterious inscription *To, Te.* The letters may stand for "Totem of the Eagle," the symbol of the Improved Order of Red Men, a fraternal society of purely American origin which was founded a decade before the Revolution. If this is so, the subject of the vane has double significance as both the image of a native American and the icon of a secret patriotic order. As if its bold profile weren't sufficiently eye catching, the artisan applied gold and deep Indian red colors on the headdress and costume.

Indian archer weather vane, maker unknown, c. 1810, painted sheet iron, height 51 inches. *Shelburne Museum.*

Jesus

Jesus did dye
For thee and I.
  —Guide for the Child,
    London, 1725

Representations of Jesus are relatively rare among the Fraktur drawings of the Pennsylvania Germans. As the great majority of the German-speaking peoples who migrated to the New World were Protestant, they avoided in their manuscript illumination direct representations of divine figures. The work of Durs Rudy, whose signed pieces include several Biblical themes, is therefore distinctive not only stylistically but in its subject matter. This scene shows Jesus after the Resurrection when he has summoned the eleven remaining disciples to Galilee, whence he sent them to make disciples of all nations and assured them of his everlasting presence. The figures are framed by classical columns incorporating tulips and other floral motifs and topped by urns from which spring more tulips and stylized flowers. In the heavens are the sun and moon, with faces that resemble those of the figures, as well as floral stars and angels. The pedestal on which Jesus stands is a reiteration of the curious classical elements which Rudy has combined with familiar Pennsylvania-German forms in the manner peculiar to his distinctive works.

Jesus and the Disciples, by Durs Rudy, probably Pennsylvania, c. 1810, watercolor and ink on wove paper, 8¾ x 6⅝ inches.
Pennsylvania German Society and the Free Library of Philadelphia.

Kitten

But the kitten, how she starts,
Crouches, stretches, paws and darts.

—"The Kitten and Falling Leaves,"
William Wordsworth, 1807

This picture of a kitten at play may have been rendered by a child who had received some instruction in drawing and watercolor painting at one of the numerous academies that sprang up in urban and rural America during the nineteenth century. The shading of the kitten's body is not confidently rendered, but the facial details, stroked on with a fine brush, and the bright, pure colors of the ball, the grass, and particularly the kitten's golden-yellow eyes make this simple composition especially arresting.

Kitten Playing with Red Ball, artist unknown, 1830-1840, watercolor on paper, 10 × 8 inches. *Old Sturbridge Village.*

L*ion*

The wicked flee when no man pursueth,
but the righteous are bold as a lion.
— Noah Webster, *The American Spelling Book*, 1793

The friendly-looking lion on William Rice's sign for the Goodwin
Tavern must have been a welcome sight to a weary traveler seeking
lodging, food, and possibly some entertainment. The creature's
bushy eyebrows and wide forehead give him an almost human
countenance, and his warm golden eyes seem to speak of the cordial
atmosphere withindoors. The chain gracefully draped across his
back forms a W, which tempts one to speculate that it might stand for
the first initial of the artist's name. *Rice* is framed by two small plants
at the bottom of the sign. Lions had been brought to America for
public display well before the sign was painted, and Rice could have
seen one himself or have adapted his rendition from a painted or
printed source. It has been suggested that the lion, as a symbol of the
English crown, is pictured enchained as a reference to the end of
British power in America.

Sign from the Goodwin Tavern, Hartford, Connecticut, by William Rice,
c. 1818, painted wood, length 74¾ inches. *Wadsworth Atheneum, Hartford, Connecticut.*

Mermaid

Who would be
A mermaid fair,
Singing alone,
Combing her hair?

—Alfred, Lord Tennyson,
  "The Mermaid," 1830

The imaginative work of Mary Ann Willson was acknowledged as early as 1894, when two of her watercolors were illustrated in a book about the Catskill region of New York. At that time the pictures were owned by Thomas Cole's son Theodore, who must also have owned a selection of the accomplished, academic Hudson River school landscapes painted by his father. Willson is reported to have lived in a log house with another woman in Greene County, New York, and to have painted a considerable number of watercolors in the first quarter of the nineteenth century, of which only twenty-two are known today. Her highly individualistic style is here embodied in the simple outline drawing and complex, random motifs executed in pure colors, some of which may have been made from berries or bricks. That a mythical marine creature should be clutching a bow and arrow is characteristic of the whimsical nature of much American folk art, and the title of the picture may be a play on the artist's name.

Marimaid, by Mary Ann Willson, 1800-1820, ink and watercolor
on paper, 13 x 16 inches. *New York State Historical Association.*

Neptune

Neptune, you shall never sink
this ship except on an even keel.

—Seneca, *Epistles*

A windswept Neptune risen to the surface of a stormy sea is a
dramatic ornament for the paddle wheel of a steamboat. The figure
appears to be younger and rather less august than the more common
stern, bearded characterization of the god of the sea, and the creature
guiding his voyage much resembles a wild pig. The sky and the sea
are gracefully united by Neptune's cape billowing up into the cloud
enframing his head. The two elements are further united by the
intersection of Neptune's arm with the lightning bolt streaking
downward from the cloud, terminating in an arrowhead which makes
its destination unmistakable.

Shield from the paddle wheel of the steamboat *Neptune,*
carved and painted wood. *The Eleanore and Mabel Van Alstyne American Folk Art*
Collection, Smithsonian Institution.

Owl

Tho' grave and solemn seems the Owl,
It is indeed a stupid fowl.

> —Alphabet card, c. 1800

Jonathan Fisher, a clergyman by profession, was also a linguist and inventor; he built his own house in Blue Hill, Maine, designed and crafted furniture for it, and made the farm implements which he used to raise crops and livestock for his family. Not the least of his talents was making pictures, which he modestly described as "a small measure of proficiency in sketching and painting." While he was a divinity student at Harvard he began his *Collection of Natural History*, a book of watercolor pictures of animals, birds, and plants, from which *The Great Horned Owl from Athens* was taken. For the pictures of species with which Fisher was not familiar he relied on natural history books by George Edwards and other British naturalist/illustrators. Although Fisher claimed that this watercolor was after an illustration by Edwards, it was undoubtedly influenced by his own observation of North American species.

The Great Horned Owl from Athens, by Jonathan Fisher, Blue Hill, Maine, 1840, watercolor on paper. *Courtesy, William A. Farnsworth Library and Art Museum, Rockland, Maine.*

PERSIMMON.

(Daimio, or Yeddo's Best.)

The Japan Persimmon, "I think will be the greatest acquisition to American fruit
ever introduced." Col. W. W. Hollister.

D. M. DEWEY'S SERIES,
COLORED FROM NATURE.

AMERICAN
FRUITS AND FLOWERS.

Persimmon

Away! Away! . . . to where purple and golden persimmons hang low from the boughs.

—Century Magazine, 1887

Although the persimmon is native to America (its name is derived from the Cree word for dried fruit), a perspicacious nursery agent would certainly have been able to tempt a rural farmer or gardener to try the Japanese variety illustrated on this plate from D. M. Dewey's sample book of fruits and flowers. Its flawless appearance and perfect shape were created with the use of theorems, or stencils, and hand colored to achieve the delicate shading and subtle highlights. Such an idealized specimen would probably have been indistinguishable from the native variety. To further tempt the prospective buyer, the plate was inscribed with an endorsement from a Colonel W. W. Hollister, who averred that the Japan Persimmon "I think will be the greatest acquisition to American fruit ever introduced."

Persimmon from D. M. Dewey, *The Colored Fruit Book for the Use of Nurserymen*, Rochester, New York, c. 1859, theorem painting, watercolor on paper. *Courtesy, Charles van Ravenswaay.*

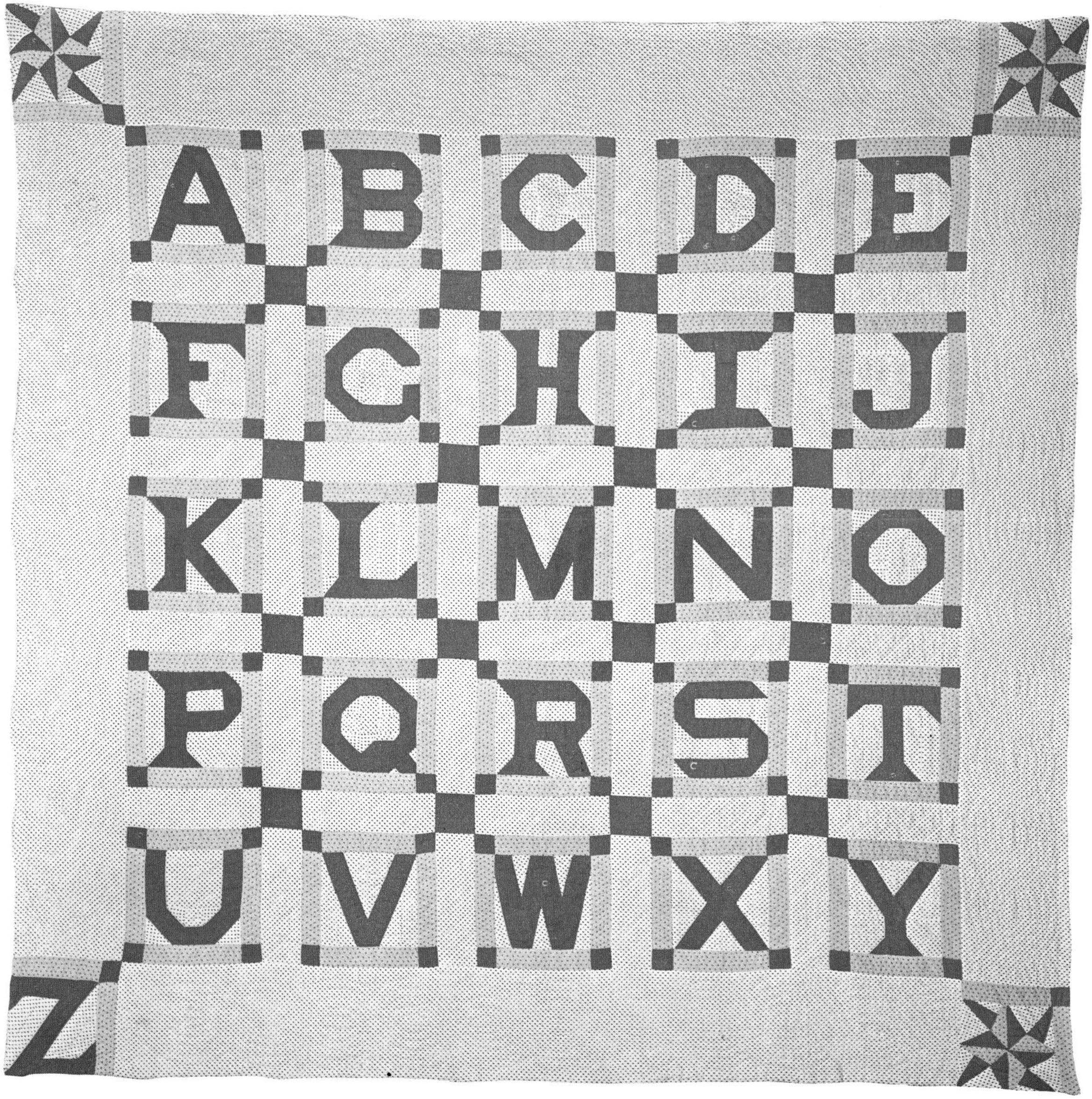
A B C D E
F G H I J
K L M N O
P Q R S T
U V W X Y
Z

Quilt

Sleep sweet beneath this silken quilt,
O thou whoe'er thou art.

    —Inscription on a quilt made 1822-1823

The thrift, ingenuity, and sense of design of the nineteenth-century American housewife who produced this original quilt are readily appreciated in the late twentieth century, but a contemporary commented in 1859, "Of the patchwork with calico, I have nothing to say. Valueless indeed must be the time of that person who can find no better use for it than to make ugly counterpanes and quilts of pieces of cotton." The technique of piecing precut strips of fabric together to form a block is best suited to a geometric design, such as the squares and stars of this example. The visual impact of patchwork quilts is a result of the careful coordination of colors and patterns. The maker of this alphabet quilt solved the obvious problem of arranging twenty-six letters in a square format by anchoring the Z in the lower left-hand corner. This must have been the result of forethought, but did she intentionally misplace the border around the star in the lower right-hand corner?

Alphabet quilt, c. 1875, found in Berks County, Pennsylvania, cotton, 80½ x 80 inches. *Private collection.*

Rose

Of ev'ry flow'r, the beauteous rose
Sweetest smells and fairest blows.

   —Juvenal Poems; or the Alphabet in Verse, 1800

As the Pennsylvania Germans adjusted to life in the New World, their art forms became less reflective of Continental European antecedents. The painted designs on documents and manuscripts, which earlier were largely subordinated to the text, became larger and more important. Occasionally Fraktur decorators created purely pictorial pieces, apparently simply for the pleasure of developing an ornamental motif without the limitations imposed by having to adapt the design to a text. This watercolor of roses is executed in the stylized manner of Fraktur decoration, with boldly drawn petals and leaves and little attempt to render perspective, although the muted shades of red and pink in the flowers have been blended to give some sense of depth. The flowers bend gracefully on thorny stems, growing up through three layers of earth which form a border that repeats the colors of the leaves, stems, and centers of the flowers.

Roses, southeastern Pennsylvania, c. 1840, watercolor on wove paper, $9^{15}/_{16} \times 7^{15}/_{16}$ inches. *Free Library of Philadelphia.*

Star

One star differeth from another star in glory.

—Corinthians 15:41

The passage from First Corinthians cited above could easily be applied to the myriad stars that appear in Pennsylvania-German decoration, in countless patterns and color combinations. Regardless of whether the star was used to represent a celestial body or was simply a geometric motif, its popularity was undoubtedly owing to its adaptability to ornament almost any form. This example from a baptismal certificate somewhat resembles the star patterns of pieced quilts made in Pennsylvania. The striking design and well-orchestrated, pure colors leave little doubt as to the proficiency of the unnamed artist, who also created the remarkable eagle pictured earlier.

Detail of a *Taufschein*, probably Northampton County, Pennsylvania, c. 1820, watercolor and ink on paper. *Free Library of Philadelphia.*

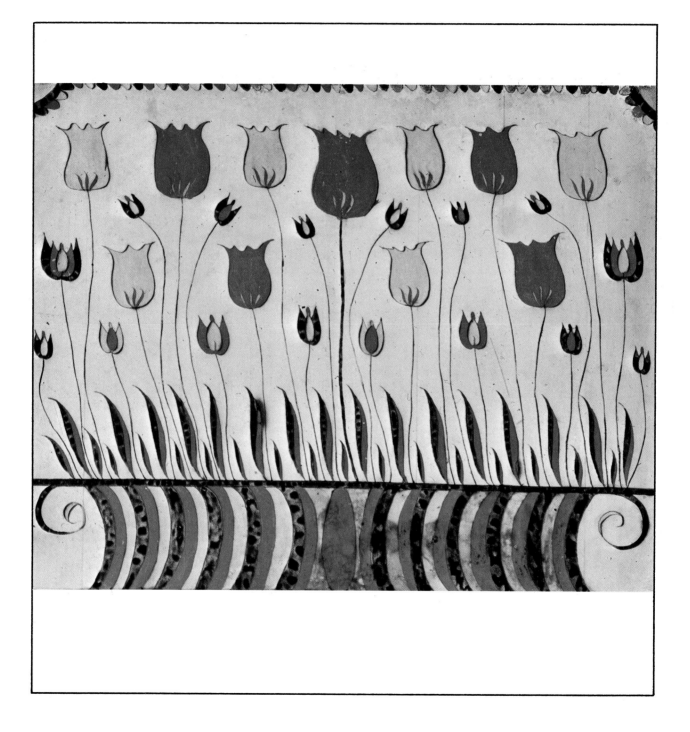

Tulip

The silks of Solomon cannot compare
With glories that the tulips wear.

— Pennsylvania-German inscription, 1807

The most popular flower motif used by the Pennsylvania Germans to ornament utilitarian objects as well as documents and manuscripts was the tulip. The simple bell shape is pleasing in itself, but it also permitted the artist to incorporate intricate geometric designs. Both highly stylized and more naturalistic tulips are found on Pennsylvania-German furniture, glassware, pottery, and metalware as well as on illuminated manuscripts. In this pictorial Fraktur the leaves and the scrolls at either end of the container are reminiscent of the calligraphic tradition from which this decorative drawing originated.

Fraktur, possibly York, Pennsylvania, 1800-1820, watercolor and ink on paper, 12⅝ x 15⅝ inches. *Henry Francis du Pont Winterthur Museum.*

Unicorn

In foreign parts
the Unicorn
Tis said is found with
but one horn.
　—Alphabet card, c. 1800

As the traditional guardian of maidenhood in medieval European lore, the unicorn is often found as part of the decoration on Pennsylvania-German blanket chests which were given to young girls for storing linens. This lean, angular fellow with his leonine tail darts out his tongue as though his collar were too tight. The floral motif over the unicorn's head and at the tip of his right fore hoof is a pomegranate, which found its way into the repertory of Pennsylvania-German decoration by way of Persian fabrics whose designs were copied in Germany in the Middle Ages. More easily identified are several incarnations of the ubiquitous tulip.

Detail of a blanket chest painted for Margaret Kern,
Pennsylvania, 1788. *Henry Francis du Pont Winterthur Museum.*

Valentine

Oh, if it be to choose and call Thee mine,
Love, thou art every day my Valentine!

—Thomas Hood,
"For the Fourteenth of February," c. 1835

It is difficult to imagine how the artist who designed and executed the intricate cutwork composition of this valentine could have misjudged the space allotted for the recipient's name, particularly since he appears to have been a gifted calligraphist. The card was made by folding a circular piece of paper into quarters and cutting out the design on concentric rings of hearts, birds, flowers, vases, and flowering vines. The cutout was then mounted on a rectangular sheet of paper to bring out the pattern. As if the cutout weren't itself sufficiently dazzling, the artist hand colored each element, carefully delineating the birds' wings, beaks, feet, and eyes and the flowers' petals, and creating the riotous patterns on the vases.

Valentine, Chester or Dauphin County, Pennsylvania, 1800-1810, watercolor and ink on paper, 16⅝ x 13 inches.
Henry Francis du Pont Winterthur Museum.

PURPLE WISTARIA.

D. M. DEWEY'S SERIES,
COLORED FROM NATURE.

AMERICAN
FRUITS AND FLOWERS.

Wistaria

Wistaria blossoms trail and fall
Above the length of barrier wall.

    —Austin Dobson, "The Story of Rosina," 1895

This frankly evocative watercolor sketch of the purple wistaria from D. M. Dewey's sample book evinces little concern with botanical accuracy. No attempt has been made to disguise the swirling brushwork, or to simulate the actual appearance of the blossoms. The American botanist Thomas Nuttall named the wistaria "in memory of Caspar Wistar, M.D. . . . . a philanthropist of simple manners, and modest pretensions, but an active promoter of science," and a fellow member of the American Philosophical Society. Nuttall noted in 1818 that the common name of the wistaria was the Carolina Kidney-bean tree, owing to the resemblance of its seeds to the "smaller kind of Kidney-beans." The gardener and seedsman Thomas Bridgeman, a contemporary of D. M. Dewey, asserted that the American wistaria "should be planted in every garden with other creepers, or to run up the trees in shrubberies, according to its natural habit."

Purple Wistaria from D. M. Dewey, *The Colored Fruit Book for the Use of Nurserymen,* Rochester, New York, c. 1859, watercolor on paper. *Courtesy, Charles van Ravenswaay.*

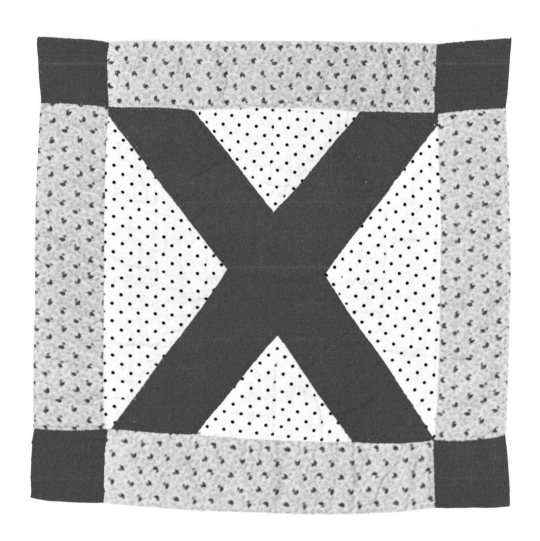

X

X in first place is eXceedingly rare;
But it stands oft in second, and sometimes elsewhere.

　　—*Tiny Tots' ABC,* 1898

X as a decorative motif occurs in fretwork friezes on fine case furniture made in the eighteenth and early nineteenth centuries as well as on chair backs; was randomly stitched in samplers; and appears on stenciled floors and walls in nineteenth-century homes. In alphabet books X usually stood for the Persian king Xerxes, a popular figure in nineteenth-century juvenile literature, or for Xantippe, the shrewish wife of Socrates, who served as an example of how not to behave. Here, of course, X represents the twenty-fourth letter in the alphabet quilt pictured earlier. From this detail one can see the carefully stitched panels that formed the block on which the letter was appliquéd with tiny, carefully spaced stitches.

Detail of an alphabet quilt of c. 1875 found in Berks County, Pennsylvania, cotton. *Private collection.*

Youth

There was a youth, and a well-beloved youth,
And he was an esquire's son.

  —"The Bailiff's Daughter of Islington,"
    traditional ballad

One could invent a very amusing tale about a lad who got all dressed up in his Sunday best and strolled off with a rooster under his arm, but the true story has gone to rest with the boy and the artist who painted his portrait. The rooster may have been the subject's pet, but his undeniable contribution is a very bright note in an otherwise basically blue and white composition. The portrait of the unnamed boy is attributed to Jacob Maentel, an immigrant from Kassel, Germany, to whom are attributed hundreds of watercolor portraits painted in York County, Pennsylvania, and New Harmony, Indiana, between about 1800 and 1842. The wispy forelock, ruffled collar, and beautifully modeled face are characteristic of portraits of boys attributed to Maentel. Though the lad is stiffly posed and stands impossibly erect on a mound of earth that appears to be floating in space, his likeness is captivating and personable.

Boy with Rooster, attributed to Jacob Maentel (w. c. 1800-1842),
watercolor on paper, 7⅞ x 5¾ inches. *Henry Francis du Pont Winterthur Museum.*

Zebra

The zebra is the most beautiful, as well as the wildest, most timid, and untameable animal in nature.

—Thomas Bewick, 1791

The wildness and swiftness of the zebra described by eighteenth-century naturalists made it a popular subject for illustration in nineteenth-century alphabet books and other children's literature. The familiar equine form with its exotic markings, here rendered colorfully by Jonathan Fisher for his *Collection of Natural History,* must have moved Americans as it did Bewick, who in 1791 remarked that the pattern of the zebra's hide was "so beautiful and ornamental that it would at first sight seem rather the effect of art than the genuine production of nature."

For his watercolor of the zebra Fisher depended on an illustration by George Edwards. He noted in his book that the zebra rendered by Edwards in 1751 was "Drawn from a stuff'd Skin in the Royal College of Physicians, London." The Englishman first saw one of these exotic creatures, in his own words, "at the palace of his late Royal Highness Frederick Prince of Wales, at Kew . . ." To Fisher and other Americans, however, the zebra must have seemed a fantastic beast.

The Male Zebra, by Jonathan Fisher, Blue Hill, Maine, 1795, watercolor on paper. *Courtesy, William A. Farnsworth Library and Art Museum, Rockland, Maine.*